Weekend Wisdom

Weekend Wisdom

*Home advice, tips and timesavers
to make your life easier
from
The Daily Telegraph readers*

*Introduction by
Eric Bailey*

Robinson
IN COLLABORATION WITH
THE DAILY TELEGRAPH

Robinson Publishing Ltd
7 Kensington Church Court
London W8 4SP

First published by Robinson Publishing Ltd 1998
Selection and editorial material © *The Daily Telegraph* 1998
Textual copyright © Various. All rights reserved.

A copy of the British Library Cataloguing in Publication Data
for this title is available from the British Library

ISBN 1-85487-578-7

Edited and designed by
OutHouse Publishing Services
Line-drawings by Annette Findlay

Printed and bound in Great Britain

Disclaimer
The following tips have been sent in by readers of
The Daily Telegraph's Weekend section and are not endorsed
in any way by either the Publishers or *The Daily Telegraph*.

Contents

Introduction

When I look at an empty plastic milk bottle, I see an empty plastic milk bottle. Not Laurence Ekblom of London, however. He sees roof insulation. He has 2,000 of the things, caps screwed *firmly* on, laid out between the joists of his London home. It seems to make sense: the plastic must be a poor conductor of heat – or is it the air?

Whatever, Mr Ekblom now benefits from two warm glows – the first courtesy of his plastic milk bottles, and the second because he has exercised his ingenuity, an elemental impulse that, even in this power-assisted era, beats in all of us. His is a classic Weekend Wisdom.

It is true of *The Daily Telegraph* in general and the Saturday Weekend section in particular that its readers are immensely responsive. Any story that arouses sympathy, interest or derision is likely to engender a surprising amount of mail and, in the case of sympathy, significant amounts of money as well. So when Weekend Wisdom – take-away tips printed in a neat circle and dotted throughout the Weekend section – was invented, and we requested help on 'food, wine, gardening, country matters or life in general', we knew enough to prepare for a minor avalanche.

The best were jaw-droppingly simple: 'Turn cans of beans upside down before opening and the beans will fall out cleanly.' Yes! Of course! So why had the rest of us spent our whole lives opening tins of beans in the normal fashion, then shaking them to get the last few out, invariably causing collateral damage to a decent shirt? Weekend Wisdoms can make you feel unutterably stupid.

Some were funny: 'Never go to bed on a quarrel; clear the decks for the next one.' Some are not for the fainthearted: 'Berry stains disappear if a lighted sulphur-tipped match is passed in front of them' – but this is the wisdom of real life, not of the escape clause and the prissy hazard warning. Some have been handed down through families as carefully as Grandad's cufflinks: 'Where there's tea, there's hope.' That one was sent in by a vicar, but submissions have come – by post, fax or, often, e-mail – from a librarian at the Bodleian Library, Oxford, and from numerous grand houses, where thrift is generally endemic. Certain objects became the leitmotifs of Wisdom: old pairs of tights, avocados, talcum powder, film canisters, wire coathangers and, of course, plastic drink bottles. Naturally, many Wisdoms arrive on recycled Christmas cards.

Just occasionally, a Wisdom evokes the feeling that the author might have wandered too far into the dangerous wastelands beyond the perimeter of our consumer society. Who, after all, would really want a 'novelty doorstop' comprising an old bubble-bath bottle filled with cat litter? Should you really bake 'fun cakes' in sandcastle buckets? Yet these too must be considered soberly, for who knows when lateral thinking becomes sheer eccentricity? And, however apparently absurd, they spring from the Weekend Wisdom rubric which becomes ever more relevant: Reuse, Recycle, Rethink.

Whether Wisdoms always work is another tricky issue. If you bury a hard avocado in flour overnight, is it really ripe the next morning? If you sleep with a bag of corks in your bed, will you never suffer from cramp? If you use a piece of eggshell to pick up another fragment in the white, will it actually draw the fragment to it? I don't know – and frankly I don't care. The point is not to submit Wisdoms to some scientific examination, but to celebrate the variety of knowledge and of that wonderful natural resource, common sense. And, of course, belief, because many Wisdoms rely on a certain degree of confidence in their efficacy – 'If you burn your fingers, touch your earlobes and the pain will vanish', perhaps a useful tip for the person engaged in eradicating berry stains.

This collection celebrates all these things by publishing some of the boxloads of wisdom that we did not have space for in Weekend. I am deeply grateful to those readers who allowed their suggestions to be used here. Their warm glows are richly deserved.

Eric Bailey
Weekend Editor
The Daily Telegraph

Around the House

Has a clumsy party guest spilt red wine on your carpet? Quickly and liberally apply white wine to stain. Shampoo later as normal.

Mrs M Levett, Farnborough, Hampshire

Remove claret stains by rubbing them with a rag soaked in sherry.

Anne Hodge, Isle of Arran

Fresh berry or currant (black, red, raspberry, etc.) stains vanish miraculously when a lit sulphur-tipped match is slowly moved over them.

M Yannicosta, London

To remove red wine stains from tablecloths: stretch the stained area over a bowl, sprinkle with dry borax, pour hot water through. Wash as normal.

Mrs J M Ackroyd, Pudsey, West Yorkshire

Mud on the carpet? Sprinkle with salt, leave for a few hours and vacuum the salt and the mud away.

Mrs Susan Young, Sherborne, Dorset

Remove small marks and stains from a carpet by rubbing with a ball of damp cotton wool. Magic – brings up the pile like new.

Jill Worth, Hindhead, Surrey

∽

You can remove biro or marker pen stains from household objects using hairspray. Test an unseen area first.

Mrs Ghulam Zohra, London

Put a small amount of Brasso on to a cloth and rub on to stains or rings on antique furniture. Allow to dry. Polish off with beeswax furniture polish.

Mrs S Groom, Nr Chichester, West Sussex

Use Swarfega to clean polished furniture dulled by constant use, then repolish with wax polish.

Mrs J M Ackroyd, Pudsey, West Yorkshire

If you spill grease on a dining table, quickly smother the spot with salt to prevent the grease from sinking into the wood.

Mr G Ireland, Bettws Newydd, Monmouthshire

Cover spilt candle wax with brown paper and apply a hot iron to remove wax.

Miss S Scutt, London

Vinegar wiped over furniture before polishing gives an extra shine.

Mrs B R Taylor, Helston, Cornwall

To clean brass, use HP Sauce, then shine with half a lemon dipped in salt.

Joan Tailby, Bognor Regis, West Sussex

Clean brass with white spirit.

G Kilby, Minehead, Somerset

Keep brass bathroom taps looking good for years by cleaning with a small amount of *mild* washing-up liquid, and rinsing with cold water!

Mrs Maureen Wayman, March, Cambridgeshire

Loosen a stiff jar lid by immersing the lid in hot water or under a hot tap for a few minutes.

Mrs Ghulam Zohra, London

A thin layer of petroleum jelly on the thread of a screw-top tube or jar will help to stop it sticking – ideal for glue containers.

Brenda Davies, Winscombe, Somerset

To remove a stubborn screw-top lid from a jar, simply stretch a rubber band tightly around the lid and twist.

Mr B Patrick, Beccles, Suffolk

Remove stiff bottle tops easily by wearing rubber gloves.

Mrs J Whiteley, York

Whenever the rubber ring in your pressure cooker becomes hard, soften it by pouring on hot water and giving the ring a little pull.

Mrs N McBrier, Belfast

To remove stains from the kitchen sink, fill with hot water, add a cupful of washing soda, and then leave for a couple of hours. Stains will wipe away easily.

C Bignell, Wilmslow, Cheshire

Cut clear plastic lemonade bottles in half to store odds and ends. Use the top end as a funnel.

C C H Dewey, Herne Bay, Kent

To unblock a sink, pour down a cup of thin bleach and leave for forty-five minutes.

Thelma Bradford, Coventry

To make light work of greasy pots and pans, first spray them with white vinegar, then wash them as usual. You'll use less washing-up liquid as well.

Maureen Chattle, Nr Royston, Hertfordshire

Soak burnt or hard-to-clean saucepans in washing powder overnight and they will dishwash or wipe clean easily.

Mrs K Donaghey, Oxford

15

Clean roasting tins, racks and the like easily by putting them into a bin liner, tossing in an eggcupful of household ammonia, tying up the bag and leaving it in the garden overnight. In the morning, take out the tins and all the grease, grime and carbon will come away very easily. Works even on years of burnt-on grease.

Jill Worth, Hindhead, Surrey

Soak burnt saucepans in cold tea overnight. Easy to clean the next day.

Mrs T Gregory, Exmouth, Devon

To completely remove tea stains from inside cups, fill with hot water, add one denture cleaning tablet, and leave overnight. Rinse thoroughly.

John Mellor, Stockport, Cheshire

The best way to clean glass vases is to use crushed eggshells. Swill around with water, rub them with fingers over bad patches. Result – sparkling vases.

Mrs A J Prior-Willeard, Shalbourne, Wiltshire

To remove scratches from glass, gently rub with toothpaste.

G Giddings, Poole, Dorset

To give your glasses and crockery an extra sparkle, wash in water with a dash of vinegar!

G Cooke, Taunton, Somerset

If glass tumblers are stuck together, fill the top one with cold water and stand the bottom one in hot water.

Mrs B R Taylor, Helston, Cornwall

Swirled with a little water, dry rice will clean discoloured glass containers.

Sylvia Emms, Leatherhead, Surrey

If you are moving, use old phone-book pages to wrap glass and china.

Mrs E M Corby, Croydon, Surrey

To stop rust forming on a steel-wool scouring pad, after use squeeze out the excess moisture and then wrap it in kitchen foil.

Mrs A Whatford, Truro, Cornwall

Use an old cleaned toothbrush for cleaning difficult mouldings or handles in the kitchen.

Mrs Ghulam Zohra, London

Keep pot scourers, brushes and other cleaning pads permanently in the dishwasher. This will provide handy storage while ensuring hygiene by a regular cleansing cycle.

B M Fruen, Winchester, Hampshire

To remove traces of rust from the blades of knives, scissors or tools, rub them with half an onion dipped in sugar.

Mrs M Raymond, Glasgow

If ivory or bone handles are yellowed, lay them in a sunny place for several hours.

Gillian Johnston, Macclesfield, Cheshire

Clean tarnished silver forks by running them through the lawn – quick, cheap and effective.

Mrs S A Dutton, Eydon, Northamptonshire

To sharpen scissors, use them to cut a piece of aluminium foil.

Mrs Susan Debusmann, London

Lost a small earring, contact lens, or similar object too small to see? Put an old pair of tights over the hose of your vacuum cleaner and sweep the area.

Mrs R D Chamberlain, Shrewsbury, Shropshire

If it is likely to snow heavily in your area, keep your snow shovel *inside* the house, not down the garden in the shed.

C Bright, Exeter, Devon

Wash out and dry thoroughly empty bottles of character bubble bath. Fill them with new cat litter granules to make novelty doorstops for children's rooms.

A Roberts, Milford Haven, Pembrokeshire

Cut a supposedly empty plastic washing-up liquid container in half and you will find sufficient liquid for at least *half a dozen* more washings-up.

Mrs J Read, High Wycombe, Buckinghamshire

To pick up a tiny fragment of broken glass, carefully wipe over the area with a damp piece of kitchen towel.

Mrs G Blake, London

Strip an old umbrella of all material, fix a strong nylon cord around the spokes, and hang the umbrella upside down to dry flowers, vegetables or washing.

Mrs E M Corby, Croydon, Surrey

Rub a pencil lead over sticky zips and newly cut keys which do not fit into keyholes. The graphite acts as a lubricant.

Mr M G Stevens, Chertsey, Surrey

Sprinkle cornflour on the damp pages of a book, then brush it off several hours later after the moisture has been absorbed.

Mrs M A Firth, Pontefract, West Yorkshire

Keep a golf ball in your kitchen. Press it down on tinfoil-topped milk bottles for easier opening.

Mrs B M Rowlands, Cheltenham, Gloucestershire

Need temporary extra worktop space in the kitchen? Pull out a drawer and place a tray over the top.

L C Mills, Maidstone, Kent

If wrapping a large gift (for example a hamper) buy a paper tablecloth to use as a jumbo sheet of wrapping paper.

Martin W Robertson, Heston, Middlesex

Leave messages for the milkman in a screw-top jam jar. They will never blow away or get wet in their watertight jacket.

Jill Worth, Hindhead, Surrey

Tube of toothpaste finished? Cut the end off and you'll see there's a lot left still to use.

L Ruddock, Folkestone, Kent

A corner cut from a used envelope and slipped over the page of a book makes an excellent bookmarker.

Mrs D Leslie Williams, Bridgend, Mid Glamorgan

Place CDs in the freezer overnight to give a brighter, clearer sound.

Brian M Stratton, Liphook, Hampshire

To prevent a candle wobbling, wrap a narrow strip of clingfilm around the bottom until it fits snugly into its holder.

Mrs S J Stonier, Emsworth, Hampshire

Before lighting candles, place them in the freezer for three to four hours. They will then burn more evenly and for longer.

Alice Carey, Chiseldon, Wiltshire

To prevent candles from dripping, place them in the refrigerator for half an hour before you use them.

Mrs P Walker, Wokingham, Berkshire

If you are thinking of buying a conservatory, add the cost of blinds or solar control film. Without them the heat in sunny weather makes them uninhabitable.

Mr Denis H Ashworth, Church Stretton, Shropshire

When not using your ladder secure it to the wall with a chain and padlock – deters burglars.

Angela Watts, Hutton Rudby, North Yorkshire

Fill small glass containers with water and place them on top of radiators. The water evaporates to humidify your room when the central heating is on.

Mrs Ghulam Zohra, London

A temporary cure for condensation: a few drops of washing-up liquid on a piece of kitchen roll applied to the condensation. Works wonders.

J Keigwin, Barry, Vale of Glamorgan

To reduce condensation in windows, place a dish of salt on the window sill. The salt will absorb the moisture.

Elaine Gallagher, Camberley, Surrey

Avoid smelly dustbins by wrapping up raw fish-heads, etc and putting them into the freezer until refuse-collection day.

Barbara Cox, Plymouth, Devon

Put cat litter in the bottom of swing bins to absorb any odorous liquid that may leak through the bag.

Clinton Buckoke, Rayleigh, Essex

Rid hands and work surfaces of smells of fish, onion, etc by rubbing them with dry mustard and washing as usual.

Mrs Susan Young, Sherborne, Dorset

To keep the refrigerator smelling sweet, squeeze lemon or lime on to kitchen paper and place it at the bottom of the refrigerator. Change the paper every ten days.

Elaine Gallagher, Camberley, Surrey

Several charcoal briquettes placed in your refrigerator or freezer will stop odours from developing.

R Goddard, South Croydon, Surrey

To deodorize 'oniony' hands, first wet them then 'wash' them with sugar. Magic!

Mrs Angela Phillips, Bradford on Avon, Wiltshire

To prevent wheelie-bin liners slipping down into the bin, use clothes pegs to clip the liner on to the rim of the wheelie-bin.

Mrs J Beechey, Hull

When a thermos flask is empty and not in use, sugar lumps placed inside will stop it smelling musty.

B A Mellor, Harrogate, North Yorkshire

A burning candle will reduce the smell of cigarette smoke.

Catherine Douglas, Stroud, Gloucestershire

∽

Silicone spray-polish keeps double-glazing tracks running smoothly.

V Lowe, Devizes, Wiltshire

For smear-free windows, clean them with water and vinegar and wipe over with a rolled-up newspaper.

Elizabeth Stacke, London

∽

Citrus peel (orange, lemon, grapefruit etc), dried overnight in the bottom oven of an Aga makes excellent firelighters.

Mrs Katherine Brazier, Canterbury, Kent

To clean glass fire-doors on wood burners or other stoves, use a damp sponge and some ash from the fire and then finish by rubbing with newspaper.

Barbara Willett, Launceston, Cornwall

A piece of raw spaghetti makes a useful taper for lighting pilot lights on anything that is difficult to get to with a match.

Mrs S Dowle, Wallasey, Merseyside

Dip the tips of kindling sticks in a little paraffin overnight to ensure successful firelighting.

Mrs M Savile, Kilham, East Riding of Yorkshire

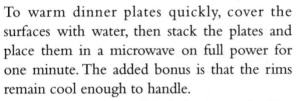

To warm dinner plates quickly, cover the surfaces with water, then stack the plates and place them in a microwave on full power for one minute. The added bonus is that the rims remain cool enough to handle.

Mrs Marie Borodenko, Sevenoaks, Kent

To avoid creasing table mats and tray cloths, store them wrapped round the discarded cardboard tubes from kitchen towels.

Mrs P D S Linton, Hexham, Northumberland

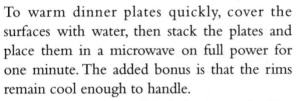

When defrosting a refrigerator or freezer, place an ordinary fan in front and defrost in fifteen minutes – cheap, quick and clean.

Bernard Wells, Holt Pound, Hampshire

After defrosting your freezer and refrigerator, coat all the ice-forming metal parts with glycerine to ensure that the ice will slide off next time.

Nancy Borland, London

∽

The elasticated tops of old tights or trouser socks make excellent, large, soft rubber bands.

Edwina Hazelton, Bournemouth, Dorset

Is your adhesive tape tearing? Or won't it run? Ten seconds in a microwave will cure it.

J M Rushton, Totnes, Devon

Temporarily restart a ball-point pen by holding the nib in an open flame for a few seconds.

Elizabeth Stacke, London

Having trouble starting a new roll of Sellotape? Warm it − placing it in the pocket of a coat you are wearing will do.

Mrs P Sheldon, Rustington, West Sussex

An envelope stuck down with egg white cannot be steamed open.

Mrs P A Gregory, Cheltenham, Gloucestershire

Dried-out felt-tip marker pens can be made as good as new by standing them in food colour overnight.

J Leigh, Hereford

Do not throw away punctured rubber gloves – cut them across in strips to make useful elastic bands of varying sizes.

Mrs M Saunderson, Crawley, West Sussex

An elastic band makes an excellent bookmark – and it won't fall out.

W Sheppard, London

29

When washing clothes in a handbasin, a residue of suds is always left behind. Run a bar of soap under the hot tap. Suds gone!

Marion Dewar, Nr Trowbridge, Wiltshire

Money-saving tip. To get the last drop of washing liquid from the plastic bags, cut the bag down three sides and put it in with the washing.

Mrs J M Brown, Weston-super-Mare, Somerset

Prevent tights from tangling and socks from going missing during a washing cycle by placing them in a pillow case before loading them in the washing machine.

Helen Nicoll, Linlithgow, West Lothian

If your washing dries to exactly the right damp state for ironing, but you cannot do it immediately, put it in the freezer.

J A Reynolds, Okehampton, Devon

Removing excess water from woollies: roll with a rolling-pin after sandwiching them between towels.

Angela Watts, Hutton Rudby, North Yorkshire

To keep pairs of socks separate in the laundry: wrap each pair in a shower-curtain ring, leaving the feet free to allow water to get to them during wash cycle.

Angela Watts, Hutton Rudby, North Yorkshire

Don't want to buy a baby bath for the new arrival? Put baby in a plastic laundry basket in the big bath.

Mrs M Hopper, Haywards Heath, West Sussex

To get rid of loo smells, just light a match!

Mrs E Chandler, Isfield, East Sussex

To avoid a bathroom full of steam, run cold water into the bath before hot.

Mrs J Holmes, Farmsfield, Nottinghamshire

Keeping new soap in the airing cupboard hardens it and lengthens its life.

Mrs Daphne Andrews, Clifton, Bristol

To get rid of bubbles in the bath after a bubble bath, just sprinkle talcum powder on them.

D Infield, London

To remove limescale from baths, etc, rub with a piece of lemon and leave for fifteen minutes before rinsing.

S Martyn, London

To prevent bathroom mirrors from steaming up, run one to two inches of cold water before turning on the hot tap.

Mrs J Connolly, Hove, East Sussex

Keep a bottle of washing-up liquid near your bath. Add a squirt to the water before you let it out - avoids tide-marks.

Hilda Moorhouse, Peterborough, Cambridgeshire

Clean the lavatory bowl with Coca Cola!

N Price, Baydon, Wiltshire

To make gliders on plastic curtain track move smoothly, spray with furniture polish containing silicones.

Mrs J Rowe, Clacton on Sea, Essex

Buy longer curtains than needed - allow for shrinkage and make matching ties.

Mrs M F Clay, London

When making dining-room curtains, buy extra fabric to make a matching tablecloth.

S M Atkinson, Croydon, Surrey

To weight curtains, simply stick 1p coins on to sticky tape and cover with tape; then slip through bottom hem of curtain.

Mrs Jean Dallas, Penzance, Cornwall

Covering a cushion with a polythene bag enables stretch covers to be put on easily.

Mrs P A Gregory, Cheltenham, Gloucestershire

If there is a dirty mark on your upholstery, use shaving foam on it for quick removal.

Mr G Ireland, Bettws Newydd, Monmouthshire

Remove chewing-gum from carpets by freezing it with an ice-cube. The gum becomes brittle and cracks away easily.

V Lowe, Devizes, Wiltshire

To remove marks or stains from carpets and upholstery, add one dessertspoonful of malt vinegar to 300ml of lukewarm water, then dab the area concerned.

Rosalind J Battershill, Beverley, East Riding of Yorkshire

Preserving the life of a carpet. Move large furniture regularly so that it does not make unattractive dents. If these do occur, leave an ice-cube to melt in the dent, let it dry and then vacuum the spot.

Angela Watts, Hutton Rudby, North Yorkshire

∽

Wash a dirty feather duvet casing one half at a time: shake the feathers down to one end, tie it up tight, then wash and dry the top half. Repeat for the other end.

G James, Bishops Waltham, Hampshire

When putting a cover on a duvet, secure the corners with a clothes peg before shaking out.

Mrs G Roe, Pinner, Middlesex

∽

Large, cheaper commercial reels of thread can be used on domestic sewing-machines by placing them over a smaller reel.

Mrs D Marsh, Welling, Kent

If you find your thimble does not fit properly, gently blow into it before you put it on your finger.

Sylvia Emms, Leatherhead, Surrey

Be environmentally friendly, use vinegar to clean your kettle. Boil the vinegar in the kettle and leave it for twenty minutes before rinsing out well. Repeat if necessary. It is as good as any commercial descaler.

Mrs F Garland, Romsey, Hampshire

Never go to bed on a quarrel – clear the decks for the next one.

L Vale, Hawkwell, Essex

If in the middle of an argument with your wife or partner you find yourself winning, apologize immediately.

Ian Baglee, Leigh, Lancashire
(34 years married)

Forget the harm that anyone has done to you and forget the good that you have done to others.

Anne Croucher, Tunbridge Wells, Kent

Touch paperwork once: deal with it, file it, or bin it.

Adrian Talbot, St Jean du Gard, France

Anyone can do anything, they say, but one thing noone can do is everything.

E M Guyver, Chipping Campden, Gloucestershire

When you get to the end of your tether, tie a knot in it and hold on.

Mrs Lucy Cooper, Nr Eye, Suffolk

Deal with the faults of others as gently as with your own!

Mrs Maureen Wayman, March, Cambridgeshire

Life is something that happens while you make other plans.

G James, Bishops Waltham, Hampshire

Clothes & Accessories

To remove chewing-gum from clothing, place the article in the freezer until solid. The gum will peel off easily.

Mrs Sutcliffe, Prestbury, Cheshire

Neat washing-up liquid applied to grease stains on silk, followed by usual washing, will remove marks.

Mrs J M Ackroyd, Pudsey, West Yorkshire

If grease, oil or gravy is spilt on clothes, coat thickly with talcum powder, leave to dry, brush off and wash normally.

C Blakeborough, Stockton on Tees, Cleveland

Has pollen from the lovely yellow lilies stained your washable clothing? Soak the stained item in cold water in sunlight – indoors or out.

Mrs D Whittle, Bolton, Lancashire

Remove pollen stains from clothes by laying a strip of Sellotape over the marks and then lifting the tape.

J Hold, Northampton

Windscreen cleaning-fluid will remove beach tar from shoes and hands.

R G Sheldon, Willingdon, East Sussex

Dab sherry onto stains left on clothes by spilt red wine.

G James, Bishops Waltham, Hampshire

Remove ink from clothing by soaking in milk before washing.

Melanie Warwick, Chiseldon, Wiltshire

Remove marks from satin shoes with bicarbonate of soda applied with a dry, or slightly damp, clean cloth.

Elizabeth Shaw, London

If you wear shoes that rub your heels, rub a candle round the inside of the heel rim and you'll have no more trouble.

Mrs J Nicholson, Exeter, Devon

If your new shoes are too tight, stretch them by pushing tightly rolled balls of wet newspaper into the toes. Leave until dry.

Mrs B Clark, Hilton, Cambridgeshire

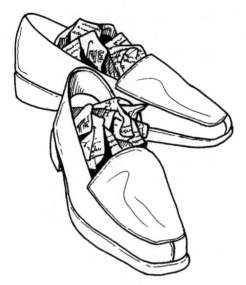

An infallible way to dry the inside of wet shoes or rubber boots is to insert crumpled newspaper, changing it once or twice after a few hours.

Michael Boardman, Coltishall, Norfolk

Stretch leather shoes with potatoes.

N Price, Baydon, Wiltshire

If you intend to have your expensive leather shoes repaired at one of the key-cutting and shoe repair shops, rather than by a traditional cobbler, first have the shop cut you a spare key to your front door – if the key doesn't fit, take your shoes elsewhere.

G Giddings, Poole, Dorset

Secure shoelaces must have a reef knot (left over right and right over left) embedded within the bow – only granny knots come undone!

E Hathaway, London

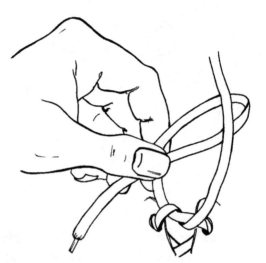

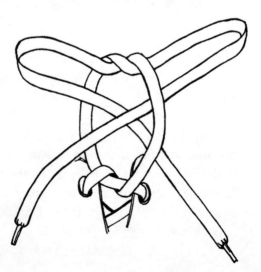

To prevent shoelaces from coming undone, pass one end over and under the other twice and pull tight before making the bow.

Mrs E Swinton, Bishop Auckland, Durham

If you get a ladder in your tights, dab the ends of the ladder with clear nail varnish and it will not get any bigger.

Miss C Antlelt, Wrexham

Use Sellotape for emergency repairs to drooping hems on skirts or trousers.

Mrs J M Ackroyd, Pudsey, West Yorkshire

Trousers that have become shiny on the seat can be revived using a flannel dipped in turpentine and rubbed over the affected area.

Brian M Stratton, Liphook, Hampshire

Use Velcro to restore the fluffiness of mohair garments that have become flat after washing.

D Blandford, Oxford

Remove pilling from knitted articles by carefully stroking them away with a safety razor.

E J Clack, Bedford

Sticky car-park tickets are excellent for removing fluff, hairs, etc from dark clothing. Peel off the paper and dab.

Mrs M Page, Deal, Kent

Rub the insides of wooden drawers with scented candles to keep clothes smelling good and to act as an insect repellent.

Mrs C Campion, Walsall, West Midlands

Save empty perfume bottles, remove stoppers, and tuck under the lining paper of your lingerie drawer. The perfumes have finished, but the memory lingers on for some months.

Mrs P Fraser-Mitchell, Swaffham, Norfolk

To preserve white, delicate Christening robes, and similar items, pack in white tissue, then cover with more tissue to prevent yellowing.

Angela Watts, Hutton Rudby, North Yorkshire

Cut the feet off an old pair of tights. Use to cover shoes when packing – saves clothes from getting marked.

Mrs B G Gittins, Mudeford, Dorset

When packing clothes, fold them over rolled-up plastic bags instead of tissue paper, as the bags stay more springy and so help to prevent creases.

Mrs B Martin, London

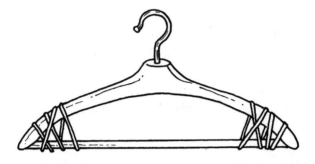

To stop clothes slipping off hangers, wind thick rubber bands back and forth across the ends. Post-office rubber bands are just right.

Mrs G Passmore, Exeter, Devon

To prevent woollens slipping off plastic hangers, attach pieces of velcro in strategic places on each hanger.

Mrs B L Lloyd, Ipswich, Suffolk

Clothes that are likely to run should be soaked in cold water to seal the dye and prevent colour loss.

Darryl Thomson, Swindon, Wiltshire

Keep a label from the yarn used to make your hand-knitted garments – you may need to refer to the care instructions.

M Brooke, Staunton, Gloucestershire

Handwash woollens in cold water with a dash of washing-up liquid. Cold rinse twice. Economical, and the woollens are soft and do not felt.

Mrs J Hobbs, Eastbourne, East Sussex

Bicarbonate of soda softens hard water – add a dessertspoonful to water when handwashing delicate woollens.

T H White, Stroud, Gloucestershire

It is easier to unpick knitting with a needle a size smaller than the one used to knit it.

D Blandford, Oxford

Putting tights in the deep freeze strengthens them.

Mrs B E Evans, Berkhamsted, Hertfordshire

Nylon stockings will last twice as long if you wear a pair of cotton gloves when putting them on.

Mrs P Barham, London

Before ironing, moisten clothes in the tumble drier.

Andy Poulton, Swindon, Wiltshire

Newly ironed clothes crease easily — always leave them hanging up for a few days before packing for a holiday.

Irene Tyson, South Bents, Sunderland

For a perfect finish when ironing silk blouses or shirts, leave them in a plastic bag in the freezer for a couple of hours first.

C Lane, Neston, South Wirral, Cheshire

For knitted garments that cannot be ironed: dampen the article and place it flat on the ironing board. Cover with a dry towel and use large books or other heavy items as a press.

K Green, London

Clean silver jewellery (and chrome bath fittings) with toothpaste.

N Goodfellow, Burford, Oxfordshire

Clean diamonds with Coca Cola.

N Price, Baydon, Wiltshire

Use a silk handkerchief or scarf to clean your spectacles.

D B Pearson, Birmingham

To colour-code and keep together pairs of earrings, attach them to lengths of woven tape five centimetres wide, then suspend the tape inside a cupboard door or store in a box.

Mrs J Anniss, Heathfield, East Sussex

Always buy good shoes and a good bed, because if you're not in one you'll be in the other.

Mrs A E Kennerley, Burntwood, Staffordshire

DIY

To mend a cracked dish, boil it in sweet milk for forty-five minutes. The crack will then be welded and hardly visible.

Barbara Verdie, Banstead, Surrey

When gluing broken china, grease round the edges of the break with petroleum jelly. This stops any surplus glue setting as it oozes out from the join. Wipe off with a damp cloth.

Ms S Balcon, Inveraray, Argyll

Strain old household paint through the foot end of an old tight.

Mrs G Edam, Nr Chichester, West Sussex

When painting, cover roller trays with foil first. Throw away the foil to leave the tray clean after the job is done.

Susan McFadzean, Swansea

When DIY gloss painting, wrap the brush tightly in clingfilm overnight. No need to clean the brush until the job is finished.

Mrs Timothie Cook, Nr Harlow, Essex

Use a razor blade for removing paint from windows.

G Giddings, Poole

To keep paint brushes in new condition, slip a rubber band over bristles after cleaning. Leave the band in position until next use.

J D McDonald, Puddletown, Dorset

Slip your roller paint tray into an inside-out plastic carrier bag before pouring in the paint. When finished, peel off bag – no tray to wash.

Mrs F Sykes, Driffield, East Riding of Yorkshire

Having painted a door and allowed it to dry, rub the edges with a candle. The wax prevents the door from sticking.

Jamie Ambrose, Richmond, Surrey

When doing home decorating, place half an onion, cut side up, inside the room. It will help to take away the smell of paint.

Mrs M Dolphin, Berkhamsted, Hertfordshire

If painting the stairs, paint alternate steps one day and the remainder the next, thus enabling the staircase to be used all the time.

J Reeves, London

When painting window frames against the light, hold an old magazine against the glass, close to the frame, to stop the glare.

W R Walsh, Harrow, Middlesex

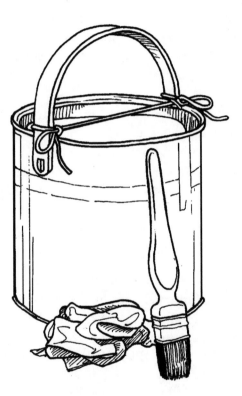

Tie a piece of string between the paint pot handles and use it to remove any surplus paint from your brush. This also provides a rest for the brush.

John Harmar-Smith, London

Store an opened paint can upside down, so no skin forms on the surface of the paint.

Annette Findlay, Swindon, Wiltshire

Reduce heat loss. To stop draughts, press Blu-Tack over the keyholes in exterior doors.

Audrey Wilson, Scarborough, North Yorkshire

Draughts: to proof windows that are not being opened in winter, use clear liquid sealant. This will set to a rubbery consistency. When the weather warms up, just peel off the sealant.

Mrs J Lojik, Shipley, West Yorkshire

Before redecorating, cut the bottoms off the spindles of internal door hinges. Afterwards, if a door should need removal, tap out the spindles, instead of spoiling paintwork.

Philip Ditton, Croydon, Surrey

If you are the victim of theft, fire or flood, take photographs or a video of the damage to your house and contents to help with your insurance claim.

Brenda Davies, Winscombe, Somerset

To save water, and cash if on a meter, place a plastic meat container (from your supermarket) in your cistern under the void for the float.

R V Emery, Axminster, Devon

When decorating a room that is higher than it is wide, tint the wall above the picture rail a shade darker than the lower part.

Brian M Stratton, Liphook, Hampshire

Don't fix your television aerial to the chimney; put it inside the loft. It lasts years longer and is safer to reach and adjust.

Mrs S J Bloor, Newquay, Cornwall

It is much easier to fix wood screws if you first rub the thread with soap.

Mrs Marilyn Beckett, Congresbury, Somerset

To protect your hands when hammering, hold the nails with a clothes peg.

A Crow, Wolverhampton

Dipping screws in petroleum jelly makes them easier to remove later.

Mr J Morgan, Quorn, Leicestershire

When nailing thin wood, flatten the nail point slightly to avoid splitting the wood.

Dave Tolfree, Towcester, Northamptonshire

If you have squeaky floorboards, sprinkle talcum powder or French chalk down and around the joints.

Tony Buck, Needham Market, Suffolk

Place a cross of masking tape on to the wall prior to knocking in a picture hook, to prevent the plaster from cracking.

Mrs S Graham, Lamorna Cove, Cornwall

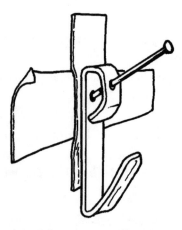

To drill to an exact depth, put masking tape on to the drill bit to mark the place where you want to stop drilling.

Graham Napper, Andover, Hampshire

To protect your saw from damage to the teeth, or yourself from injury, cut plastic wire-ducting to length, then slide over tooth-edge of the saw.

John Miles, Rugby

Your log-saw seems blunt. Reverse the blade so you will be cutting with the end that has had less use.

Anthony Warner, Tunbridge Wells, Kent

If a saw sticks, rub a candle on to the blade. Ideal for damp wood.

Graham Napper, Andover, Hampshire

When wallpapering, spour the paste into a roller tray and use a roller. This spreads paste quickly and evenly.

Mrs S Young, New Barnet, Hertfordshire

When repapering a room, write down the number of rolls used on a thin pasted strip and stick the strip on top of the door frame.

Bert Twiddy, Carshalton, Surrey

Trouble in wiring a plug? BRown: Bottom Right, BLue: Bottom Left and the remaining wire to the earth pin at the top.

Dr W G Taylor, Scarborough, North Yorkshire

When cutting open bales of hay or straw, cut the string next to the knots and pull it through. This prevents snagging and the string slips round easily.

Mrs Sarah Middlewood, Kilham, East Riding of Yorkshire

Trick of the trade: changing windscreen-wiper blades is infinitely easier if first you turn off the windscreen wipers.

Mr M Murray, Barrow-in-Furness, Cumbria

Food & Drink

For fat-free gravy add several ice cubes to warm meat juices. The fat will solidify around these and can easily be removed.

Mrs Jo Stables, Selby, North Yorkshire

To reduce the fat content of standard or lean mince even further, before cooking place the thawed/fresh meat in boiled water for five to ten minutes, then drain well.

Mrs Ghulam Zohra, London

Stock and gravy cubes will keep dry and crumbly if stored in the refrigerator.

Mrs J O Flynn, Louth, Lincolnshire

Marinate meats and fish prior to freezing. They are then ready to use once you have defrosted them, and the flavour and moisture content is better.

Gay Page, London

Perfect pork crackling: remove from joint, microwave on high for about three minutes, and leave to stand for a further three minutes.

G Giddings, Poole, Dorset

When freezing minced meat, put the mince in a bag, flatten it, then store in the freezer. This saves space, and the meat defrosts more quickly!

Mrs M Mackenzie, Alicante, Spain

Marmalade-making tip: to produce more juice and make the removal of flesh and pith very easy, put one fruit at a time in very hot water for two minutes.

Mrs Patricia Long, Bickington, South Devon

When making marmalade, squeeze the juice from the oranges (saving the pips) then use a food-processor to chop the remaining pith and peel.

Mrs P Ellerman, Southburgh, Norfolk

Before pouring newly made marmalade into jars, add a knob of butter to the preserving pan to disperse all the scum.

Judy Cheshire, Taunton, Somerset

When potting jam or marmalade, dip the wax discs in a little brandy to prevent mould and guarantee the preserve's keeping quality.

Mrs M A Goodall, Winchester, Hampshire

When making jam or marmalade, put a 20p coin in the bottom of the pan to prevent the mixture sticking.

Susan Truscott, Truro, Cornwall

To retain the texture, colour and nutrients of fresh stirfry vegetables, microwave them first in a covered dish. This will reduce cooking time in the wok.

Mrs Ghulam Zohra, London

To cook perfect rice: first soak the washed rice in cold water for at least thirty minutes, or leave overnight. Drain, then cook as instructed on the packet in boiling water with one tea-spoonful of oil.

Mrs Ghulam Zohra, London

Use an egg slicer to slice fresh button mush-rooms quickly and evenly.

Barbara Verdie, Banstead, Surrey

When preparing packs of green beans etc, stand the pack on end and get all the 'tops' together then cut through the whole lot. Do the same for the other end.

Mrs M Poole, Huddersfield, West Yorkshire

A tablespoon of milk in cauliflower water keeps the flower white.

Miss D Myers, London

Put a slice of lemon in the pan with your potatoes to keep them white.

Susan Mercer, Winsford, Cheshire

Add bicarbonate of soda to green vegetables during cooking – prevents yellowing.

K Bradford, Bromley, Kent

Put residue from fresh fruit and vegetable juice on the compost heap.

Eryl Humphrey-Jones, London

Peel vegetables over a piece of *The Daily Telegraph*. When finished, fold up paper and remove peel and paper parcel neatly to bin or compost heap.

G Brady, Exeter, Devon

Wash fresh strawberries *before* hulling. They will then keep their flavour.

Mrs Ghulam Zohra, London

To keep broccoli, cut a slice off the end of the stem, and place the vegetable stem-down in some water – it will keep fresher for days.

Mrs Geraldine Dyke, Birmingham

To keep potatoes from sprouting, store an apple with them.

Mrs L M Hill, Bournemouth, Dorset

To keep coriander fresh, remove main stems and store in an airtight jar in the fridge.

G Giddings, Poole, Dorset

Celery stalks separated, placed in cold water for fifteen minutes, dried and placed in a freezer bag will keep crisp for two weeks in the refrigerator.

Mrs L V Skeats, Solihull, West Midlands

Do not store bananas in a mixed fruit bowl: their presence speeds the decomposition of other fruit.

D Blandford, Oxford

Fully ripe avocados will keep perfectly for two to three weeks in the refrigerator salad box if wrapped in kitchen foil, shiny side inwards.

Mrs Carol Grant, Sturminster Newton, Dorset

To encourage avocado pears to ripen, place them in a polythene bag with a soft apple.

Mrs Ruth Horsfall, Huddersfield, West Yorkshire

To keep watercress fresh, store it upside down with the leaves in the water.

Miss S Scutt, London

To keep lettuce or watercress fresh in the refrigerator, place in a polythene bag containing a piece of coal. Twist to close bag.

Mrs J M Ackroyd, Pudsey, West Yorkshire

Recycle bubble wrap by using it to line refrigerator drawers. Fruit and vegetables keep fresh for longer because of the improved air circulation around them.

S A Dey, London

To keep a half-used tin of tomato purée fresh, pour on a little olive oil to cover the surface, then store in the refrigerator.

V Lowe, Devizes, Wiltshire

If you have left-over tomato purée, freeze it in teaspoonfuls in an ice-cube tray. The cubes can be used as and when necessary straight from the freezer (one or more at a time).

Mrs Jennifer Cohen, Cheadle, Cheshire

The skin of a garlic clove will fall away if you first slice off the tip then tap the clove hard with side or handle of the knife.

Elizabeth Shaw, London

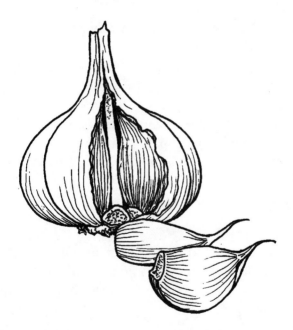

To remove the skins from baby onions, make small slits in the skins and place in boiling water – the skins will come away easily.

Miss S Scutt, London

To avoid tears when peeling onions, prepare them under water.

Anne Hodge, Isle of Arran

You will shed fewer tears if you cut the root end of the onion last.

Mrs F M Gorman, Eton, Berkshsire

∽

A dry crust of bread in cabbage water will absorb the smell.

Miss D Myers, London

When cooking green vegetables, add a bay leaf to the water to stop them smelling.

Mrs E M Joslyn, Carshalton Beeches, Surrey

∽

A pea-sized knob of butter in your saucepan will stop your potatoes from boiling over.

Mrs J R White, Wistaston, Crewe, Cheshire

To stop the contents of a saucepan from boiling over, grease the whole of the inside of the lid with any household fat – margarine, lard etc.

Mrs P Gregory, Aveley, Essex

When boiling potatoes, to prevent the water from boiling over when your back is turned, add a peeled and sliced carrot to the saucepan.

Roger Sykes, Woodbridge, Suffolk

When boiling potatoes, a splash of vinegar in the water prevents them from breaking up.

Mrs Sue Hempstead, Horsham, West Sussex

Revive limp lettuce, spinach, etc by placing them in cold water to which a small piece of coal has been added, for half an hour.

Mrs Elizabeth Rose, Christchurch, Dorset

To crisp a wilted lettuce, cut $1/4$ inch off the base with a steel knife and place the lettuce upright in a bowl of water.

M D Sansom, London

Limp bunches of coriander will revive dramatically if left in a bowl of lukewarm water for half an hour or so.

Mickie Wynne-Davies, Oxted, Surrey

If you have some left-over wine, pour it into ice-cube trays and freeze. It's ideal for adding flavouring to stews or gravy

Andrea Hazeldine, Greenford, Middlesex

For soup at dinner parties, make croutons more attractive by cutting them out with small cocktail cutters

V Lowe, Devizes, Wiltshire

If too much salt has been added when cooking soups, casseroles etc, add one or two roughly quartered potatoes to soak up the salt. Remove potatoes once they have softened.

Mrs Ghulam Zohra, London

Use strained low-fat yoghurt as a healthy alternative to cream in cooking. This works especially well in soups, meat and fish dishes.

Mrs Ghulam Zohra, London

Improve your usual sage and onion packet stuffing mix by roughly chopping an onion into it. Cook in the usual way.

Audrey Marsden, Glastonbury, Somerset

Dry any left-over sticks of celery in a slow oven and use them for flavouring soups and stews. They will keep for weeks.

Mrs J Jeffery, Cupar, Fife

A small fruit or vegetable net from the super-market makes an excellent lifter for boiled or steamed puddings.

Mrs O R Barrett, Swindon, Wiltshire

Instead of muslin, use a well-washed tights leg to strain jellies through.

Mrs G Edam, Nr Chichester, West Sussex

Use up surplus Christmas alcohol for soaking dried fruit, dates, etc to add to cakes and steamed puddings.

Mrs T Foulkes, Amlwch, Isle of Anglesey

When using a spice such as cinnamon for making pears in red wine and other similar dishes, mix the cinnamon with sugar before adding it to the liquid. This stops the cinnamon from separating.

Mrs B K Lane, Epsom, Surrey

When stewing rhubarb, drop in a cube of raspberry jelly. This adds colour and an extra tropical flavour.

Jenny Farmer, Westbury-on-Trym, Somerset

To reduce the acidity of rhubarb, stew it in cold tea.

Anne Hodge, Isle of Arran

To prevent bananas from discolouring in a fruit salad, put them in a container and cover with boiling water. When the skins turn black, remove them, allow them to cool, peel and use them.

Mrs E Turner, Newcastle-upon-Tyne

To prevent bananas from going brown in fruit salad, submerge them whole, unskinned, in a bowl of cold water for at least one hour before cutting.

Sue Brannen, Scarborough, North Yorkshire

When cutting up apples, pears or bananas, a squeeze of lemon juice will stop them from turning brown.

Mary Mackinnon, Leatherhead, Surrey

Don't throw away your old sugar tongs, they're ideal for stalking strawberries.

Mr G F Forbes, Port Glasgow, Inverclyde

Excess whipped double cream can be piped into rosettes on to a tray, then frozen and used later to decorate desserts.

Edith Brack, Birkenhead, Wirral

Before decorating a cake with icing, lightly sprinkle flour over the top – this prevents the icing from running down the sides.

Elaine Gallagher, Camberley, Surrey

If your cooked cake won't come out of the tin, stand the tin on a damp cloth for a few minutes.

Mrs M Eason, Loughborough, Leicestershire

An apple placed in your storage tin with your cakes will prevent the cakes from becoming dry.

Mrs Margaret Durkin, London

An easy way to fill a piping bag: put it nozzle down in a jug and fold the bag over the rim. This leaves both hands free for filling it up.

Angela Watts, Hutton Rudby, North Yorkshire

To make moist cakes (especially sponge cakes), place an oven-proof glass of water on a corner of the baking tray when you bake.

Kazuko Wood, Windermere, Cumbria

To keep scones light and springy, place an eggcupful of water alongside when warming them up in a microwave.

Mrs Angela Baker, Oxford

Sprinkle water on the top of fruit cakes before baking the prevent them from cracking.

Mrs R Shaw, Glossop, Derbyshire

Roll out pastry on floured clingfilm – very easy to move around when thinly rolled out.

Judy Portway, Stowmarket, Suffolk

When cutting slices of pizza use kitchen scissors – much easier than a knife!
Mrs P Ellerman, Southburgh, Norfolk

To cut out a recipe from the newspaper, take a pin, score around the recipe. Lift recipe out.
Miss M E Arderne, Nr Manchester

Save waste, cut costs. Approximately every six weeks check dates on food labels. Then have fun concocting new recipes using the food nearing its expiry date.
Mrs J Blackmore, Marlow, Buckinghamshire

To prevent a mixing bowl from slipping when you are whisking, place a damp dishcloth underneath it.
Mrs Maureen Wayman, March, Cambridgeshire

Dry rice prevents boiled sweets from sticking.
Sylvia Emms, Leatherhead, Surrey

Freeze grated cheese and breadcrumbs and use as required.
Helen Brown, Leighton Buzzard, Bedfordshire

Put nuts in the freezer for one day before you intend to crack them open. They are more likely to come out of their shells whole and are easier to tackle.

V Coppen, Liddington, Wiltshire

When your honey or syrup hardens and sets, take off the lid and put the jar in a saucepan of boiling water. The contents will desolidify in minutes.

Mrs Geraldine Dyke, Birmingham

Before serving Brie cheese, flash it under the grill for ten seconds to enhance the flavour and consistency.

Adrian Sinclair, Enfield, Middlesex

To stop cheese from becoming mouldy, store it in the refrigerator in an airtight container with two lumps of sugar.

Mary Mackinnon, Leatherhead, Surrey

Chill very fresh bread before you slice it. It is less likely to split or break.

V Coppen, Liddington, Wiltshire

Keep demerara sugar soft and separate by placing it in an airtight container with a piece of bread.

Mrs Joan Cockerell, Stamford, Lincolnshire

A vanilla pod in a jar of caster sugar makes vanilla sugar.

Zoe Sargeson, Marlborough, Wiltshire

Use pastry cutters to cut out shapes from sandwiches for children's parties.

E J Clack, Bedford

To squeeze a lemon, pierce its pointed end with a skewer, wriggle the skewer round inside (to break up the flesh) then squeeze. This is a clean efficient way to get lots of juice out of a lemon.

Barbara Purdom, Beccles, Suffolk

To keep lemons fresh for a long time, place them in a jar of cold water. Change the water three times a week.

Jill Jones, Waltham Saint Lawrence, Berkshire

A little sugar in salad dressing takes the acidity out.

Zoe Sargeson, Marlborough, Wiltshire

A few grains of raw rice added to the salt in a pouring-type salt container ensures that the salt remains dry.

Mrs E Christie, Oxted, Surrey

Before opening a tin of baked beans or such, turn the tin upside down: the beans will fall out cleanly.

Mrs J Parker, Whitehaven, Cumbria

When breaking eggs into a bowl, elusive fragments of broken shell can easily be removed with a metal spoon previously dipped in cold water.

Mrs Kathleen Daubney, Fareham, Hampshire

A boiled egg will spin freely when twirled on a hard surface; a raw one will wobble around slowly.

H-F von Claer, Pervenchères, France

Crack the shell immediately after hard-boiling an egg to prevent dark circles forming around the yolk.

Miss G Connacher, Whitley Bay, Tyne & Wear

Store eggs pointed end down. They stay fresher for longer.

Mrs T Gregory, Exmouth, Devon

To test the freshness of an egg, place in a glass bowl of water: if the egg stands up on its end, it is stale; it if it lies across the bottom of the bowl, it is fresh.

D Brady, Bolton, Lancashire

To stop eggs from cracking when boiling, add a dead match to the water.

A M Harasymiw, Warley, West Midlands

One egg well beaten is worth two unbeaten.

Mrs M McDowell, Hillingdon, Middlesex

For quick preparation of lemon slices, for drinks, first cut a lemon lenthways, then hold the halves together and slice from end to end.

K Green, London

To use up halves of lemons, simply slice and open freeze them. Store the slices in the freezer and use whenever needed for cocktails and drinks.

Elaine Gallagher, Camberley, Surrey

Remove excess gas from champagne or sparkling wine by either dropping a wooden chopstick into the bottle or holding it in the glass – more effective that the traditional swizzle stick.

Elizabeth Shaw, London

To keep champagne fresh and fizzy for more than a day after opening, just refrigerate with a silver-plated dessertspoon hanging in the neck of the bottle.

Jane Ward, Weybridge, Surrey

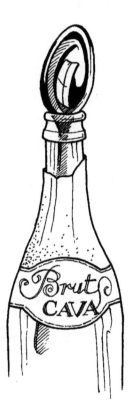

Tap the top of a can of fizzy drink before opening – prevents it from fizzing over.

G Giddings, Poole, Dorset

Half-fill an ice-cube tray with orange juice. When frozen, top up with another juice (or water) and freeze – ideal for children's drinks.

Elizabeth Bracey, London

Carefully wash chocolate-box trays, fill them with water and freeze to make unusual-shaped ice cubes.

A Hazeldine, Greenford, Middlesex

To chill a bottle of white wine more quickly, add a handful of cooking salt to the surrounding ice cubes in the ice bucket.

Mrs Barbara Joyce, Swindon, Wiltshire

Keep bubbles longer in partly used plastic bottles of tonic water, etc, by squeezing the container until the contents reach the bottle tops. Replace the screw top tightly and refrigerate.

Mr J Goodhew, Gillingham, Kent

As a safety measure, leave the cork on the corkscrew after opening wine.

E. Watkins, Stratford upon Avon, Warwickshire

Keep a few pieces of dried orange peel in the tea caddy. It upgrades the cheapest tea - the best becomes nectar.

Mrs H M Edwards, Carlisle, Cumbria

Instead of buying coffee filters: take a piece of kitchen towel, fold into four and make a pocket.

Miss W Prowse, Plymouth, Devon

Keep your ground beans in the freezer for a fresh cup of coffee every time.

Mrs A Sutcliffe, Prestbury, Cheshire

Two ways to an indulgent, stress-free life: always eat bread fresh, but don't read today's news until tomorrow.

Mrs J Pilgrim, Yeovil, Somerset

Gardening

Small film canisters make neat, airtight containers in which to store seeds saved for the garden. They are easily labelled and dated too.

Mrs K Hooper, Emsworth, Hampshire

When flowering bulbs in the garden are finished, if they have to come up and you are short of space, store them in old tights.

Miss W Prowse, Plymouth, Devon

Tubes of newspaper filled with compost make ideal individual seed containers for sweetpeas. They can then be transplanted directly into the garden.

Mrs J Baptie, Sheffield

Cut discarded cardboard tubes from inside carpet rolls into short lengths. Use for potting seeds or thinning out seedlings.

John Miles, Rugby, Warwickshire

Pour boiling water on parsley seed before sowing to hasten germination.

Mrs D Edwards, Salisbury, Wiltshire

When selecting runner bean seeds for planting, drop them into a jar of water. Only plant those that sink straight to the bottom.

Mrs S K Smith, Swansea

A golf tee makes a good dibber when pricking seedlings.

Mrs J G Charles, Weston-super-Mare, Somerset

To germinate reluctant seeds, prepare the soil by pouring on boiling water. When it is warm (not hot), sow the seeds and cover them with a cloche cut from a six-litre milk bottle.

Mrs M R Clark, Canterbury, Kent

Sweetpea seeds germinate within five days if placed between two polystyrene trays lined with moist tissue in a sealed plastic bag in warmth.

D & D M Pepperday, Batley, West Yorkshire

Confusing trays of seedling beans, I paired climbing with dwarf plants by each cane. The crop was the best ever on my small patch.

Joan Storrar, Roselea, Lydney, Gloucestershire

Set some of your cooking coriander seeds and chilli pepper seeds (thoroughly dried) in compost for bunches of fresh coriander and white-flowering chilli plants.

Mrs M Rushton, Thurmaston, Leicestershire

Sow seeds singly by using the dampened end of a matchstick to pick each one up.

Marjory H B Gray, Guildford, Surrey

Use egg boxes as mini flower-pots or seed trays: they can be planted directly into the soil.

Mrs D Henderson, Bushey, Hertfordshire

When cutting back vines, keep the prunings and cut them into short lengths below a bud. Put them in a jar of water on a warm window sill. When roots appear, pot up as normal.

Dena Bryant, Luton, Bedfordshire

Oasis used to arrange flowers can be reused to root shrub cuttings. Remember to keep the oasis wet, then insert the cuttings. When the roots have formed, pot the cutting up in growing compost.

Mrs S Bain, Wakefield, West Yorkshire

Sprinkle bicarbonate of soda on garden paths and crazy paving to kill weeds in crevices.

Mrs Ghulam Zohra, London

Washing soda dissolved in boiling water kills moss on driveways.

Mrs Marilyn Beckett, Congresbury, Somerset

Use boiling water to kill weeds growing in awkward crevices. No residues or side effects.

F N Curwood, Bolton, Lancashire

Sprinkle salt on paths and crevices to get rid of weeds and grass.

Mrs C Meadows, Chelmsford, Essex

To kill dandelions, sprinkle salt on the leaves and within two weeks they should dry up and die.

Mrs F E Avery, Stockport, Cheshire

A French marigold planted in pots and hanging baskets will keep greenfly away from the other summer bedding plants.

Mrs J M Simpson, High Peak, Derbyshire

A clove of garlic planted by the base of a rose bush will guarantee freedom from greenfly. The garlic acts as an organic systemic insecticide.

Mrs J M Simpson, High Peak, Derbyshire

Leave some 2p pieces by an ant run, and the ants will leave the infested area.

H W Sumpner, Southport, Merseyside

If your garden suffers from moles, locate the entrance to their tunnel and pour oil from a sardine tin down it. It works!

Sheila Evill, Ingatestone, Essex

Use empty upturned coconut shells in the garden to trap slugs, snails and woodlice.

Mrs Betty Dutton, Dover, Kent

An all-round smear of Vaseline, an inch from the tops of your patio pots, will prevent slug damage to your treasured hostas.

Mrs G G Nicholls, Stourbridge, West Midlands

Slug killer: leave a few drops of beer in the can, lay the can on its side in the garden. Slugs can't resist the beer!

M Dawson, Windermere, Cumbria

To keep slugs and snails from eating runner bean plants, use crushed and baked egg shells round each plant instead of poisonous slug pellets.

Mrs Mary Mackinnon, Leatherhead, Surrey

Bury empty yoghurt pots up to their rim, fill with beer. After a few days they will be full of slugs. An ideal, organic slug trap.

Mrs S R Roberts, Chester

Bran sprinkled around newly transplanted seedlings should protect them from slugs and snails and is harmless to other animals or birds.

Carol A Jarvis, Harpenden, Hertfordshire

For a completely organic and guaranteed way of keeping slugs away from prize saplings, simply scatter holly leaves around the base, thus preventing their ravenous advances.

Bernadette Byrne, Naas, Co Kildare, Ireland

Dry used teabags, put a few drops of eucalyptus oil on them and place them on garden beds. Cats hate the smell! Renew when necessary.

Mrs J Jackson, Halifax, West Yorkshire

To keep cats off your garden, scatter mothballs, or hang mothballs on sticks placed around favourite plants.

Mrs P Cooke, Hayling Island, Hampshire

To stop cats fouling, sprinkle finely chopped orange peel over your flowerbeds. Cats hate the smell of orange peel. It definitely works.

Mrs Rachel Ufton, Dorchester, Dorset

To keep cats off your garden, put some camphorated oil on used tea-bags around the plants. The teabags will later make good compost.

Mrs P Cooke, Hayling Island, Hampshire

To keep cats from bare patches in flower beds, push in rose prunings. Any that take root are a bonus.

Mrs M E Everard, Lymington, Hampshire

To deter cats in the garden, scatter some sprigs of prickly holly over the beds. They are not as unsightly as orange peel, and will last much longer.

Mrs M Navin, Cambridge

Fill plastic lemonade bottles with water and place in the garden – cats will not soil near fresh water.

Simon Hay, London

∽

Put a used teabag into the bottom of a plant pot to prevent the soil falling through the drainage holes.

Mrs A Swanbury, Lowestoft, Suffolk

To help retain moisture when potting-up cuttings, place a used tea-bag at the bottom of the pot.

Mrs Denis, Leicester

Put broken-up polystyrene into the bottom of patio pots to a quarter of the depth of the pot. Saves on compost and waste.

Mrs R Davis, Camberley, Surrey

Save used wine corks for rattling garden-fence panels. Cut broad corks diagonally lengthwise, making wedges. Works a treat for quiet sleep!

Mary Green, Bolton, Lancashire

Old interlocking clay roof tiles (thrown away by the skipful by roofing contractors) inserted vertically edge to edge around a flowerbed make a fantastic border and cost nothing.

M J Howarth, Boston, Lincolnshire

Surround gro-bags containing tomato plants with a dry wall made out of old house bricks. When the tomatoes have finished, tip out the gro-bags and plant spring bulbs in the soil.

Barbara Quirk, Southampton, Hampshire

Use a jam funnel to make refilling the wild-bird feeder easier.

E Sayers, Chepstow, Monmouthshire

Fit four feet of flexible plastic tubing over the electric cable adjacent to a hedge trimmer. This prevents the cable from slipping between the blades and being cut.

Jill Wren, Bradford, West Yorkshire

When putting compost on your garden ready for spring, beware of disturbing hedgehogs sleeping in the compost heap.

Maureen Chattle, Nr Royston, Hertfordshire

To stop people from injuring themselves when bending over canes, which can be difficult to see amongst a border of plants etc, place empty yoghurt pots on the tops of stakes.

Angela Watts, Hutton Rudby, North Yorkshire

Bamboo canes are a great hazard in the garden. Stick your smallest potatoes on the tops of the canes to prevent accidents. They will last for a year.

Miss Barbara Eagles, Nr Malvern, Worcestershire

For staking large herbaceous border plants, use canes with a wire coathanger attached to make a circle. The circle can be moved up the canes as the plants grow, and new shoots tied in.

Mrs C Milton, Bristol

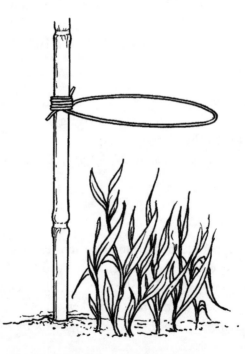

In the garden, cover the ends of canes and bean sticks with the caps from fabric-conditioner bottles, to protect eyes from injury.

Mrs Smith, Pontypool, Gwent

When a rubber glove splits, do not throw away. Use the sound fingers to put over garden canes, doubled or trebled to give added protection.

Mrs L Corcoran, Maidstone, Kent

Don't throw away laddered tights or stockings. Cut the legs into strips and use them to secure rose bushes, etc., to walls, fences or stakes. They will stretch as the plant grows.

Mrs Clare Larkin, London

To protect pond fish from herons, cut off both ends of plastic bottles and drop the remaining tubes into pond to serve as hiding-places.

Jim Doolan, Dublin

Pond too full? Fix an inclined piece of guttering so that it carries fountain spray away to absorbent ground.

Terence Parker, Salisbury, Wiltshire

In icy weather, fill a large, plastic lemonade bottle or similar with hot water and let it float in your garden pond. Replace the water at regular intervals. That way your fish will always have a breathing-hole.

Jill Worth, Hindhead, Surrey

To frostproof terracotta pots, give them a coating of PVA.

Mrs L Wesley, Wirral, Merseyside

During the winter frosts, sprinkle cooking salt on to your garden paths to help melt the ice and snow more quickly.

Mrs C M Herbert, Aveton Gifford, Devon

Cut off the tops and bottoms of lemonade or water bottles. The remaining plastic cylinder can be pressed into the soil to protect tender plants.

Mrs Mary R Wilkinson, Caldy, Wirral

Five-litre plastic bottles with the bases cut off make ideal cloches for small frost-sensitive plants. Reversed they become summer reservoirs for thirsty ones.

Mrs F Wilkins, London

To protect your greenhouse from the worst of the frost, burn a candle under an inverted clay plant-pot.

Graham Hunter, Bexhill on Sea, East Sussex

Protect any pots on the patio during winter by upending the trays to prevent water collecting and freezing when icy.

Mr G Wagstaff, Southend on Sea, Essex

An old rubber hot-water bottle makes an ideal kneeling mat in the garden.

Mrs June Charles, Weston-super-Mare, Somerset

Sugar soap is an inexpensive and environmentally sound cleaner for slippery and mossy patios, paths or backyards.

Mrs M Sadler, Chepstow, Monmouthshire

To remove slime from paving stones and paths, sprinkle them with crushed washing soda. Apply a light water spray or wait for rain.

Mrs S M Blamire, Millom, Cumbria

Melt some beeswax on to your shovel to give it a non-stick coating – snow will then slide off easily.

G Anderson, Slough, Berkshire

A stout, old ironing-board makes an ideal mobile workbench in the garden for planting hanging baskets, potting flowers, DIY etc.

Mrs M Davis, Uxbridge, Middlesex

A pair of shower caps can be useful when gardening. Slip them over muddy shoes when going indoors to answer the telephone – no more dirty floors.

Mrs B Duncan, Leeds

Before weeding scrape your fingernails across a cake of soap. When gardening is over washing is easy. No dirty fingernails.

Joan Masters, Easingwold, North Yorkshire

Smooth rough hands by washing with one teaspoon cooking oil and one teaspoon sugar. Rinse.

Mrs Peggy Lidstone, Cheriton Fitzpaine, Devon

∞

Before planting, bury a length of perforated hose wrapped in inch-thick newspaper, leaving one end protruding from the ground. Attach a funnel to the end and soak your plant regularly, using bath and waste water.

Eric Belle-Vue, Shoeburyness, Essex

If you constantly lose your garden hand-tools in the herbaceous border, paint the handles brilliant red or white.

Mrs M K Pollard, North Petherton, Somerset

After using shears and other garden implements, give them a quick wipe with an oily rag kept handy in an old margarine tub.

Mrs M Beales, Ipswich, Suffolk

Make plant labels by cutting up the lids of plastic ice-cream boxes.

Mrs G C Smith, Orpington, Kent

Before filling your wheelbarrow, point it in the direction you intend to go.

B A Mellor, Harrogate, North Yorkshire

Hoe before you can see the weeds, then you will not have any.

Miss E M Day, Bedford

When someone is born, gets married, or dies, plant a tree for them in a special place.

Peter Murphy, Basingstoke, Hampshire

Health & Beauty

To speed-up the drying of nail varnish, after twenty minutes run your nails under cold water.
Miss C Antlelt, Wrexham

Nail varnish will stay fresh if the bottle is kept in the refrigerator.
Mrs Irene Brown, Monmouth

Press your nails into soap before tackling any dirty jobs. Wash your hands afterwards and the dirt will rinse off easily, leaving clean nails.
Mrs Jean Dallas, Penzance, Cornwall

To whiten nail tips, cut a lemon in half and plunge nails into its flesh for a few minutes.

D B Pearson, Birmingham

In the mornings, put your day's supply of medication into a clear bottle. You can see what you have to take and will not miss a tablet.

Mrs G Goves, Plymouth, Devon

My husband's hiatus hernia problem was controlled by taking porridge before going to bed. He has no more pain and sleeps without discomfort. Worth trying.

Mrs Muriel Lucock, Nr Canterbury, Kent

To banish a wart, apply the juice of a dandelion stem two or three times daily.

Mrs T Cunliffe, Chorley, Lancashire

Keep a pot plant by your computer – reduces the CO_2 in the atmosphere.

N Price, Baydon, Wiltshire

Use essential oil of tea-tree to treat fungal infections such as athlete's foot.

S Kirk, Formby, Lancashire

To clear up nappy rash: cover the rash with a little lightly beaten egg white. Works wonders.

Mrs I M Bagley, Storth, Cumbria

Hot feet or hot flushes? Fill a hot-water bottle with cold water and put it in the freezer until frozen solid. Wonderful for hot feet or to cool a pillow.

P Palmer, Grimsby, Lincolnshire

To make your expensive body lotion last, mix it with an unperfumed, cheap body lotion. You will smell great every day on a budget!

Mrs R D Chamberlain, Shrewsbury, Shropshire

Don't wear handcream on the day you give blood as it affects the finger-prick test and gives a faulty reading.

Mrs C E Constable, Heathfield, East Sussex

Use soothing garden herbs in your bath. Put them into a leg from a pair of tights, tie it to a tap and immerse the herbs in the water.

Mrs G Edam, Nr Chichester, West Sussex

Lavender oil on your pillow induces sleep.

Zoe Sargeson, Marlborough, Wiltshire

Stir four or five tablespoons of dried milk into your bath for skin like Cleopatra's.

Gloria M Sutcliffe, Beverley, East Riding of Yorkshire

Always start emptying the bath before you get out. If you slip and hurt yourself, at least you won't drown.

Mrs Eden, Edinburgh

Wash or shower using coal tar soap to keep biting insects at bay for summer evening barbeques.

M Fildes, York

∞

For really shiny hair, rinse with cold water.

Miss C Antlelt, Wrexham

To make your hair shine, wrap a silk scarf around your hairbrush and brush your hair with it.

N Price, Baydon, Wiltshire

Nail varnish remover dissolves chewing gum in the hair.

G Giddings, Poole, Dorset

If chewing-gum becomes entangled with hair, rub in chocolate and rinse out the resulting mixture.

Gavin Michael, Letham, Angus

To remove chewing-gum from your child's hair: wearing gloves, hold a piece of ice on the gum until it is frozen and then chip the gum off.

Mrs T Rooke, Guildford, Surrey

When trying to disentangle hair, start at the ends of the hair, not at the scalp.

G Giddings, Poole, Dorset

To ease discomfort caused by heated rollers, roll up hair and slide an orange stick between head and curler – this lifts the heat away from the scalp.

Margaret Lovell, London

To make a form to support a French pleat or roll: take a pair of stockings, or the legs from a pair of tights, and starting at the toes roll them together into a sausage shape. Arrange the hair over the form and secure with hairpins.

Christine Galloway, Bournemouth, Dorset

For scalded fingers, grasp the lobe of your ear. The heat will transfer to the ear, reducing the pain in your fingers. It works!

Mrs H Cooper, Southwold, Suffolk

A wet tablet of soap rubbed on to minor burns brings almost instant relief.

Mrs E Johnson, Alstonefield, Derby

Soothe burns with cold milk and apply a thick paste of bicarbonate of soda made with a little water.

J Fordham, Ruislip, Middlesex

Cucumber is great for taking the sting out of sunburn. Rub it on the affected area every few hours.

Marion Wren, Neston, South Wirral

To soothe a wasp sting, apply a red-tipped match to the area. It takes the sting away.

Miss S Scutt, London

To soothe irritation and itching from insect bites, use toothpaste.

Mrs June Shaw, Oldham, Lancashire

For wasp stings, apply vinegar. For bee stings, bicarbonate of soda.

Elizabeth Stacke, London

Use a bicarbonate of soda paste for insect bites.
G Kilby, Minehead, Somerset

To repel head lice when there is a school epidemic, aply lavender oil to a child's hairline at the nape of the neck and behind the ears.

K Green, London

To prevent a common cold from developing: when a sneeze is coming, close your mouth and sneeze through the nose.

Mrs P J Ransom, Leigh on Sea, Essex

Gargle for winter sore throat: two or three drops of lavender oil, one teaspoonful of vodka; mix with an eggcupful of water. Gargle and spit out.

D Hodson, Chichester, West Sussex

Chewing a raw onion wards off colds.
Lois Bourne, St Albans, Herts

Fill a hot-water bottle with boiling water, pour in a few drops of eucalyptus oil, close tightly, shake, open and inhale when necessary. Good for colds and sinuses.

B Pitt, Brecon, Powys

A silk scarf worn around the neck prevents sore throats.

M Popperwell, Royston, Hertfordshire

As an emergency measure, protect yourself from hayfever with a smear of Vaseline just inside each nostril.

N Price, Baydon, Wiltshire

For hip or knee problems with steep cottage stairs: half-height blocks nailed on alternate halves of each step halve the height for legs to climb.

Ray & Dickie Finucane, Liss, Hampshire

To avoid cramp in the feet or legs at night, scrub and dry a medium potato and place it in your bed. This has been tested with success for years.

Mary L Stokes, Tetbury, Gloucestershire

For cramp: rub affected area hard with cork. If you suffer from cramp in bed, keep a muslin bag containing corks in the bed.

Mrs E Crossfield, Wombourn, Staffordshire

People who suffer from cramp at night should keep a cork beside them and hold it in a clenched fist at the first sign.

Mrs G M Walker, Ilminster, Somerset

To ease night cramp in your feet, wear loose bedsocks and put in a cork, next to the painful spot.

M D Sansom, London

Before throwing away a steaming hot teabag, use it as a swab for any minor cut, graze or swelling on the hand. Very healing it is.

Godfrey H Holmes, Chesterfield, Derbyshire

To quickly cure split finger tips during cold weather, apply a cotton bud dipped in Friars Balsam, and healing takes place in a few hours.

Mr R Dudley Utting, Compton, Hampshire

Eucalyptus oil, applied freely to trapped fingers and bad bruises, eases pain and prevents the nail from coming off. No throbbing either.

Mrs R Probart, Radstock, Bath

A handful of salt in bath water easily cleans grazed knees and minor wounds.

Mrs P A Gregory, Cheltenham, Gloucestershire

The inside of an onion skin pressed over a cut will promote quick healing.

Mrs T Gregory, Exmouth, Devon

∽

To cure hiccups put a lump – or teaspoonful – of sugar in the mouth. *Do not eat it.* Just let it dissolve and your hiccups will disappear.

Penelope Carmichael, Alton, Hampshire

To stop hiccups, push your thumbs against your ears and press your little fingers against your nostrils, then swallow.

Mr B Ruffell, Braintree, Essex

Infallible, instant cure for hiccups: half a teaspoonful of white wine vinegar or malt vinegar.

John H Shaw, Greenford, Middlesex

For an instant cure to stop any bleeding in the mouth, suck half a teaspoon of brown sugar. A marvellous remedy for accident-prone children!

Mrs G Bayley, Ramsbury, Marlborough, Wiltshire

To relieve mouth ulcers. Chew the rind of a quartered fresh grapefruit, sugared if necessary. Let the juice swill round the sore spots. Repeat during the day. Painful but effective.

Mrs Pam Sinclair, Stone, Staffordshire

To remove the smell of garlic from your breath, chew a piece of fresh parsley. Not a trace of garlic will remain on your breath.

Mrs H Joucla, Bournemouth, Dorset

Cure or prevent abcesses by twice-daily rinsing, after teeth cleaning, with two drops of tea-tree essential oil, diluted in five millilitres of water.

Mary Cockman, London

To whiten your teeth, clean them with grated lemon zest on a toothbrush.

Kazuko Wood, Windermere, Cumbria

Soak dentures in a Milton sterilizing-fluid solution. It's far more effective than denture-cleaning preparations, and cheaper, too.

Angela Timms, London

Frozen bananas make great teething soothers.

Zoe Sargeson, Marlborough, Wiltshire

A dab of oil of cloves will numb toothache until you can see the dentist

Mrs C Brown, Malpas, Cheshire

Smother an aching tooth with a piece of soft white bread for temporary relief from pain.

John H Shaw, Greenford, Middlesex

Use out-of-date natural yoghurt as a revitalizing face mask.

Mrs Ghulam Zohra, London

Mix together an egg yolk, some oatmeal, almond oil and powdered milk for a nourishing face-pack. Leave on the face for twenty minutes and wash off – radiant soft skin

Anne Sutcliffe, Prestbury, Cheshire

A soft eyebrow pencil will be easier to sharpen after a few hours in a refrigerator.

Lois Bourne, St Albans, Hertfordshire

To make lipstick last longer, smooth some foundation and translucent powder on to the lips before applying the colour. Repeat.

Catherine Douglas, Stroud, Gloucestershire

To blot lipstick after applying, use a cigarette paper.

Elaine Gallagher, Camberley, Surrey

If you find that your brand new mascara is too wet, remove applicator brush and stand brush and tube separately overnight.

K Bradford, Bromley, Kent

Bleach freckles with lemon juice.

C Chandler, Gateshead, Tyne & Wear

Keep perfume and make-up in the fridge during hot weather.

Zoe Sargeson, Marlborough, Wiltshire

For a quick, natural solution to stomach ache, crush the seeds of a large black cardamom pod and chew with plenty of water. Repeat if necessary.

Mrs Ghulam Zohra, London

If you suffer from diarrhoea when taking antibiotics, eat some live yoghurt each day as it replaces the beneficial flora in the gut.

Mrs Joan Foden, Clevedon, Somerset

Relieve constipation by eating dandelion leaves.
Mrs B Grasby, Banbury, Oxfordshire

Troubled with indigestion? Eat plenty of onions.
Mrs B Grasby, Banbury, Oxfordshire

For nausea or an upset stomach, eat sliced fresh ginger.

Mrs Anne Sutcliffe, Prestbury, Cheshire

Relieve baby's constipation with orange juice mixed with a little brown sugar.

Zoe Sargeson, Marlborough, Wiltshire

An apple a day keeps the doctor away, a clove of garlic keeps everyone away.

Mr Simm, Bolton, Lancashire

Learn from the mistakes of others. You can't live long enough to make them all yourself.

B Davies, London

Keep your head, hands and feet warm to be sure,
Then the doctors and chemists will be poor.

Mrs G Soameson, London

Compliments are like perfume, to be inhaled and not swallowed.

Mrs Lucy Cooper, Nr Eye, Suffolk

Indoor Plants & Flowers

To water delicate pot plants, fill a sponge with tepid water and squeeze gently whilst moving it over the plant.

E Watkins, Stratford upon Avon, Warwickshire

Use left-over cold tea to water indoor plants – they much prefer it to tap water. You'll be amazed at the beneficial results.

Mrs P McCann, Herne Bay, Kent

After using an egg, put the eggshell in a screw-top jar filled with cold water. Use this water for indoor plants and watch them flourish.

Mrs E Gordon, Eastbourne, East Sussex

Quickly cleanse the foliage of indoor pot plants (not hairy ones) using a lukewarm shower.

Mrs Elizabeth Allison, Cupar, Fife

When peeling fresh garlic for cooking, save the skins and put them around the compost of conservatory plants. Whitefly hate garlic, and keep away.

S Graham, Penzance, Cornwall

To prevent greenfly on your house plants, bury a clove of garlic in the soil.

Mrs D Edwards, Salisbury, Wiltshire

An ailing pot plant put on top of the refrigerator and given care for a few weeks picks up well in the controlled atmosphere.

Mrs Diana Sandes, Ballyduff, Co Waterford

A copper coin placed in the tray beneath a pot plant, or pushed into the soil, will invigorate your plant. In a vase, it will make cut flowers last longer.

Angela Timms, London

When displaying spring flowers in a vase, keep irises and daffodils separate to prolong the life of both.

Mrs Ghulam Zohra, London

To make cut flowers last longer: put a teaspoon of sugar and a teaspoon of household bleach into the water.

Angela Watts, Hutton Rudby, North Yorkshire

To make cut roses last longer, dip the ends of the stems in boiling water before arranging them in a vase.

Angela Timms, London

Say farewell to tulip droop! As soon as cut, pierce the stem about an inch from the flower head with a fine pointed needle. Result, proud upstanding tulips!

Mrs D M Brown, Stafford

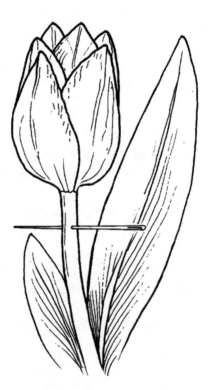

To prevent cut hellebores from wilting, slit the stems up to the flower and place in deep, tepid water. The flowers will last for days.

Pamela Morris, Southsea, Hampshire

If you place cut carnation flowers in a vase of lemonade instead of water, they will last at least three weeks.

S Bailey, Potters Bar, Hertfordshire

Arrange cut flowers in mineral water.

Angela Timms, London

A soluble aspirin dropped into a vase of cut flowers will keep the blooms fresh.

Margaret Paroutaud, Cheltenham, Gloucestershire

Put cut tulips in vase with one inch water (and top up daily). They will stand up straight and will not flop.

T Coghlan, London

To deter houseflies, include some mint sprigs in your floral arrangements.

Mrs Weir, Coniston, Cumbria

Arrange your favourite flowers in a plastic wine cooler: the even temperature will make them last much longer.

Mrs Margaret Brown, Hornchurch, Essex

The best way to clean glass vases is to use crushed eggshells. Swill around with water, rub them with fingers over bad patches. Result – sparkling vases.

Mrs A J Prior-Willeard, Shalbourne, Wiltshire

∞

However much you like house plants leave some space in the house for your husband. Plants are easier to replace.

Hanna Tomczewska, Tadcaster, North Yorkshire

Out & About

To prevent a handbag or briefcase being snatched from your car while driving, attach a dog lead to the car seat. Clip the lead to the bag.

Mrs C M Beresford, Birmingham

Keep a shoelace in your bag. Use it to tie your bag to your supermarket trolley for security whilst you examine goods and are distracted.

Mrs C M Beresford, Birmingham

Before travelling abroad, photocopy the front and back pages of your passport. Trim to size and pack separately. Helps with supplying details if your passport is stolen.

Mrs N E Hansford, Mold, Flintshire

When going away on holiday, ask a friend or neighbour to fill your bins. Then no one will know you're away.

Miss W Prowse, Plymouth, Devon

Before going abroad, list your traveller's cheques and exchange with those of your companions. Helpful if documents are stolen.

Mrs N E Hansford, Mold, Flintshire

Going on holiday abroad? Take with you a cheap calculator so that you can make conversions when bargaining or eating out.

Anne Hollier, Stoke Goldington, Bauckinghamshire

When parking in a supermarket car park, attach a ribbon to your car aerial and you'll have no problem locating your car after shopping.

G Morrison, Aviemore, Highland

Tie a balloon to the aerial of your car to help you locate the vehicle when you're parked on a large showground.

Mrs Patricia Turner, Telford, Shropshire

Driving tip: keep your wheels straight whilst waiting to turn right. If you are shunted from behind with the wheels turned, your car will be pushed into the oncoming traffic.

Mrs S B Weston, Dorchester, Dorset

A ping-pong ball hung from the garage roof so that it touches the car windscreen above the steering-wheel centre makes neat, space-saving parking easy every time.

Ian Hourston, Orkney

Place a nine-inch square of brown paper next to the skin on a child's tummy to stop travel sickness.

D Johnson, Newcastle-upon-Tyne

Always keep a soft duster immediately to hand in the car. A lot of 'fog' is inside the windscreen. Dusting also reduces glare.

Godfrey H Holmes, Chesterfield, Derbyshire

When you leave your Labrador in the car while you go into the butcher's, take the car keys with you. He's heavy enough to depress the lock buttons and lock you out.

Alice Carey, Chiseldon, Wiltshire

Save empty small plastic bottles (such as those previously used for cleansers, etc) for use as travel containers for your usual toiletries.

Mrs Ghulam Zohra, London

Ban damp towels from bathrooms/holiday luggage – dry off any excess moisture with a flannel first!

Penelope Walford, Birmingham

When visiting Third-World countries, take a squash ball with you. It will fit most plug-less basins and baths.

H-F von Claer, Pervenchères, France

Avoid constant re-packing on touring holidays. Place skirts, shirts, etc., in separate marked bags. Take them out at each stop-over, leaving the smaller items in your suitcase easily accessible.

Mrs May Gratrix, Stockton Brook, Staffordshire

When preparing for a country ramble, pack a supermarket carrier bag, split down the side, to sit on during tea and lunch breaks.

F Boden, Bristol

Save black film canisters, pierce holes in the lids and use for salt and pepper on picnics.

Mrs R F Wilkinson, Waldron, East Sussex

Put a refrigerated drink into a children's cool-bag – it will keep your lunch cold when you are at work or out rambling.

Mr J Goves, Plymouth, Devon

If you are trying to keep to a budget (or a diet), don't go shopping at the supermarket when you're hungry.

D B Pearson, Birmingham

When shopping in wet weather, take along a plastic bag – it makes a safe place for a dripping umbrella in a shop or café.

Joan Phillips, Cullercoats, Tyne & Wear

At the supermarket, exchange shopping lists with a friend and then exchange shopping at the payout, thus avoiding unplanned items.

Glenis Gerrish, Sandbach, Cheshire

Use a cheap address book to list measurements of room areas, width of curtains, etc., and carry it with you in your handbag when shopping.

Ms R Burgess, Stockport, Cheshire

Use a discarded or broken fishing-rod and reel for kite-flying. It makes control much easier than using a hand-held reel of string.

John Miles, Rugby

Always carry two large-size freezer bags and ties. When the weather lets you down, use them over shoes or as a rainhat, and when the dog lets you down use one as a glove to pick up the faeces and the other to seal the offending item.

Glenis Williams, Crewe, Cheshire

To prevent your goggles from misting up when in the swimming bath, rub the glass with a little shower gel on both sides, then rinse it off.

Mrs M Watson, Maghull, Merseyside

Let your hand tremble slightly when carrying a full beer glass some distance. This stops waves from developing, so that no ale is lost.

John Sampson, Edinburgh

Unwrap ice-lollies from the top so that the stick remains encased in paper – saves drips.

Elizabeth Stacke, London

When photographing groups, take several exposures in quick succession to have spares to give away – cheaper than ordering reprints.

Mrs J McCallum, Chelmsford, Essex

Wear woollen socks over shoes to prevent slipping on iced pavements.

Mrs C Wright, Surbiton, Surrey

If you want to succeed, find out which way the crowd is going and get to the front.

Mrs Lucy Cooper, Nr Eye, Suffolk

Before entering a high-rise lift, buy a *Daily Telegraph* and some sandwiches.

D Golden, Newton Abbot, Devon

Pets

For treating arthritis in horses, dogs and cats, give best sunflower oil: one tablespoon three times daily for large animals; one dessertspoon three times daily for medium; and one teaspoon three times daily for small. My old Alsatian and I are completely cured.

Patricia Appleby, Newton Abbot, Devon

My two dogs used to regularly suffer from Colitis. Now, instead of expensive vet's bills, they get charcoal biscuits or pills, which seem to solve the problem.

M Forbes-Buckingham, Queen Camel, Somerset

∽

Dogs that chew cabbage or cauliflower stalks have perfect white teeth all their lives and no bad breath. My Dalmatians like them at bedtime.

Mrs Mary Mackinnon, Leatherhead, Surrey

Bicarbonate of soda is an effective tooth cleaner for dogs. Apply with a damp cloth.

Elizabeth Stacke, London

Lay a jam pot on its side in a hamster's cage. It will be used as a toilet, and can be rinsed out daily. Never fails!

Brian Robbins, London

A solution of baking soda dissolved in water will neutralize the smell left by a tom cat's spray.

Judith Mayne, Bideford, Devon

For cat litter try garden peat. Not only is it cheaper and less dusty, but you can reuse it in the garden.

Mrs Joyce B Thompson, Rochdale, Lancashire

Torn-up newspaper makes a convenient and cheap filling for a cat's litter tray.

Mrs A Fuhrmann, Weymouth, Dorset

Do not throw away old wholemeal or granary bread. Toast it and use it to supplement your dog's mixer biscuits.

Bardi A Collins, Weston-super-Mare, Somerset

Recycle 200gm coffee-jar lids as pet-can saver lids. They fit exactly.

Ann Lacy, Slimbridge, Gloucestershire

When detergent fails to shift the tenacious saliva from a well-licked dog's bowl, reach for a teapot; strong tea-dregs work wonders.

Tony Whitmarsh, Ullapool, Highland

To prevent your rabbit's outdoor drinking bottle from freezing, place it in a very small jiffy bag or wrap in bubble wrap.

Mrs L Prattent, Christchurch, Dorset

If you keep young rabbits, chop their greens up small, and mix with hay to stop them bolting their food.

J Acker, Whitstable, Kent

To make a wonderful free toy for your puppy, knot together old socks and tights. It can be pulled, chased and tossed endlessly.

Mrs J Young, Buntingford, Hertfordshire

Moving house? Ensure you have your dog's tag ready and fitted on the day. Many pets go missing within days of moving to a new area.

Mrs D Lodge, Epping, Essex

If you are disturbed at night by your dog barking or scratching, use a two-way baby monitor or intercom at your bedside and shout. It works!

D Newport, Harrogate, North Yorkshire

If your kitten starts being afraid of the vacuum cleaner, carry her the next few times you hoover. Awkward but usually effective – works with babies, too!

E Hatfield, Skipton, North Yorkshire

To get rid of annoying dog hairs from carpets, wipe firmly with a damp sponge and gather up the hairs.

M Lenden, Kendal, Cumbria

To remove hairs from the carpet, use a metal dog-grooming comb with one-inch teeth. Hold it at right angles to the carpet and 'sweep' with, never against, the pile. This is far more effective than using damp cloths, gloves, etc., and it also works on upholstery.

Angela Timms, London

Use inflated balloons to keep cats or dogs off furniture or away from any objects or places you don't want them near. It works a treat.

Mrs A Davies, Bath, Somerset

When bathing your dog, wash the face and ears last – it discourages the dog from shaking before the job's done.

D B Pearson, Birmingham

Wear old rubber gloves to stroke cats and dogs and remove loose hair. Also excellent for removing pet hair from furniture.

Mrs V Thorley, Solihull, West Midlands

Avoid wet dog smells! Use old tea towels rather than bathroom towels for drying your pooch after baths or walks – much quicker and they dry quickly too.

S Graham, Penzance, Cornwall

Since rabbits groom themselves frequently and cannot vomit, hairballs can be a problem, but papaya enzyme tablets (available from health stores) keep hairballs at bay.

Rosy Dillon, Chesterfield, Derbyshire

If your dog or cat has an accident on the carpet, sprinkle the area liberally with soda water to neutralize the smell before mopping it.

B Woodwark, Lyme Regis, Dorset

My best tip for cat owners: have two large Vapora strips about the house and your pets will be free from fleas – wonderful!

Adrian Sinclair, Enfield, Middlesex

Instead of flea spray, rub a few drops of lavender oil on the nape of your cat's neck. It is more effective and acceptable.

Mrs T Mindham, Chichester, West Sussex

Try adding a piece of garlic to your dog's dinner. It helps to keep away fleas as they hate the aroma.

Andrea Hazeldine, Greenford, Middlesex

When using tea-tree-oil shampoo as a flea repellent, avoid applying to any areas that the dog can lick – tea-tree-oil is hallucinogenic.

Elizabeth Shaw, London

To remove a tick from your dog or cat, first apply surgical spirit or similar to make the tick release its grip; then use tweezers to ease the tick out.

Margaret Lovell, London

To encourage a reluctant cat to swallow a pill, lightly (and quickly) touch the tip of its tongue.

Mrs Sally Rush, Eldersfield, Gloucester

To give your cat a tablet, crush the pill, mix with butter and smear it on to a front paw. He will clean his paw and eat the tablet.

David Skeet (aged 11), Milton Keynes,
Buckinghamshire

If your cat needs a pill, insert the tablet into a spoonful of cheap fish paste.

Mrs K Sweet, Worcester

Acknowledgements

This book could not have been compiled without the help of many readers of *The Daily Telegraph*. They include:

J Acker, Mrs J M Ackroyd, Mrs Elizabeth Allison, Jamie Ambrose, G Anderson, Mrs Daphne Andrews, Mrs J Anniss, Miss C Antlelt, Patricia Appleby, Miss M E Arderne, Mr Denis H Ashworth, S M Atkinson, Mrs F E Avery, Ian Baglee, Mrs I M Bagley, S Bailey, Mrs S Bain, Mrs Angela Baker, Mrs S Balcon, Mrs J Baptie, Mrs P Barham, Mrs O R Barrett, Rosalind Battershill, Mrs G Bayley, Mrs M Beales, Mrs Marilyn Beckett, Mrs J Beechey, Eric Belle-Vue, Mrs C M Beresford, C Bignell, Mrs J Blackmore, Mrs G Blake, C Blakeborough, Mrs S M Blamire, D Blandford, Mrs S J Bloor, Michael Boardman, F Boden, Nancy Borland, Mrs Marie Borodenko, Lois Bourne, Elizabeth Bracey, Edith Brack, K Bradford, Thelma Bradford, D Brady, G Brady, Sue Brannen, Mrs Katherine Brazier, C Bright, M Brooke, Mrs C Brown, Mrs D M Brown, Helen Brown, Mrs Irene Brown, Mrs J M Brown, Mrs Margaret Brown, Dena Bryant, Tony Buck, Clinton Buckoke, Ms R Burgess, Bernadette Byrne, Mrs C Campion, Alice Carey, Penelope Carmichael, Mrs R D Chamberlain, C Chandler, Mrs E Chandler, Mrs J G Charles, Maureen Chattle, Judy Cheshire, Mrs E Christie, E J Clack, H-F von Claer, Mrs B Clark, Mrs M R Clark, Mrs M F Clay, Mrs Joan

Cockerell, Mary Cockman, T Coghlan, Mrs Jennifer Cohen, Bardi A Collins, Mrs J Connolly, Mrs C E Constable, Miss E Connacher, A Crow, Mrs Timothie Cook, G Cooke, Mrs P Cooke, Mrs H Cooper, Mrs Lucy Cooper, V Coppen, Mrs E M Corby, Mrs L Corcoran, Barbara Cox, Mrs E Crossfield, Anne Croucher, Mrs T Cunliffe, F N Curwood, Mrs Jean Dallas, Mrs A Davies, B Davies, Mrs Brenda Davies, Mrs M Davis, Mrs R Davis, Mrs Kathleen Daubney, M Dawson, Miss E M Day, Mrs Susan Debusmann, Mrs Denis, Marion Dewar, C C H Dewey, S A Dey, Rosy Dillon, Phillip Ditton, Mrs M Dolphin, Mrs K Donaghey, Jim Doolan, Catherine Douglas, Mrs S Dowle, Mrs B Duncan, Mrs Margaret Durkin, Mrs Betty Dutton, Mrs S A Dutton, Mrs Geraldine Dyke, Miss Barbara Eagles, Mrs M Eason, Mrs G Edam, Mrs Eden, Mrs D Edwards, Mrs H M Edwards, Mrs P Ellerman, R V Emery, Sylvia Emms, Mrs B E Evans, Mrs M E Everard, Sheila Evill, Jenny Farmer, M Fildes, Annette Findlay, Ray & Dickie Finucane, Mrs M A Firth, Mrs J O Flynn, Mrs Joan Foden, Mr G F Forbes, M Forbes-Buckingham, J Fordham, Mrs T Foulkes, Mrs P Fraser-Mitchell, B M Fruen, Mrs A Fuhrmann, Elaine Gallagher, Christine Galloway, Mrs F Garland, Glenis Gerrish, G Giddings, Mrs B G Gittins, R Goddard, D Golden, Mrs M A Goodall, N Goodfellow, Mr J Goodhew, Mrs E Gordon, Mrs F M Gorman, Mrs G Goves, Mr J Goves, Mrs S Graham, Mrs Carol Grant, Mrs B Grasby, Mrs May Gratrix, Marjory H B Gray, K Green, Mary Green, Mrs P Gregory,

Mrs P A Gregory, Mrs T Gregory, Mrs S Groom, E M Guyver, Mrs N E Hansford, Miss A M Harasymiw, John Harmar-Smith, E Hatfield, E Hathaway, Simon Hay, A Hazeldine, Edwina Hazleton, Mrs Sue Hempstead, Mrs D Henderson, Mrs C M Herbert, Mrs L M Hill, Mrs J Hobbs, Anne Hodge, D Hodson, J Hold, Anne Hollier, Godfrey H Holmes, Mrs J Holmes, Mrs K Hooper, Mrs M Hooper, Mrs Ruth Horsfall, Ian Hourston, M J Howarth, Eryl Humphrey-Jones, Graham Hunter, D Infield, Mr G Ireland, Mrs J Jackson, G James, Carol A Jarvis, Mrs J Jeffery, Jill Jones, D Johnson, Mrs E Johnson, Gillian Johnston, Mr E M Joslyn, Mrs H Joucla, Mrs Barbara Joyce, J Keigwin, Mrs A E Kennerley, G Kilby, S Kirk, Ann Lacy, Mrs B K Lane, C Lane, Mrs Clare Larkin, M Lenden, Mrs M Levett, Peggy Lidstone, Mrs P D S Linton, Mrs B L Lloyd, Mrs D Lodge, Mrs J Lojik, Mrs Patricia Long, Mrs J Leigh, V Lowe, Margaret Lovell, Mrs Muriel Lucock, C Lane, Mrs M Mackenzie, Mrs Mary Mackinnon, Audrey Marsden, Mrs D Marsh, Mrs B Martin, S Martyn, Joan Masters, Judith Mayne, Mrs N McBrier, Mrs J McCallum, Mrs P McCann, J D McDonald, Mrs M McDowell, Susan McFadzean, Mrs C Meadows, B A Mellor, John Mellor, Susan Mercer, Gavin Michael, Mrs Sarah Middlewood, John Miles, L C Mills, Mrs C Milton, Mrs T Mindham, Hilda Moorhouse, Mr J Morgan, Pamela Morris, G Morrison, Peter Murphy, Mr M Murray, Mrs D Myers, Graham Napper, Mrs M Navin, D Newport, Mrs G G Nicholls, Mrs J Nicholson, Helen Nicoll,

Gay Page, Mrs M Page, P Palmer, Margaret Paroutaud, Mrs J Parker, Terence Parker, Mrs G Passmore, Mrs B Patrick, Andy Poulton, D B Pearson, D & D M Pepperday, Angela Phillips, Joan Phillips, Mrs J Pilgrim, B Pitt, Mrs M K Pollard, Mrs M Poole, M Popperwell, Judy Portway, Andy Poulton, Mrs L Prattent, N Price, Mrs A J Prior-Willeard, Mrs R Probart, Miss W Prowse, Barbara Purdom, Barbara Quirk, Mrs M Raymond, Mrs P J Ransom, Mrs J Read, J Reeves, J A Reynolds, Brian Robbins, A Roberts, Mrs S R Roberts, Martin W Robertson, Mrs G Roe, Mrs T Rooke, Mrs Elizabeth Rose, Mrs J Rowe, Mrs B M Rowlands, L Ruddock, Mrs Sally Rush, Mr B Ruffell, J M Rushton, Mrs M Rushton, Mrs M Sadler, John Sampson, Mrs Diana Sandes, M D Sansom, Zoe Sargeson, Mrs M Saunderson, Mrs M Savile, E Sayers, Miss S Scutt, Elizabeth Shaw, John H Shaw, Mrs June Shaw, Mrs R Shaw, Mrs P Sheldon, R G Sheldon, W Sheppard, Mr Simm, Mrs J M Simpson, Adrian Sinclair, Mrs Pam Sinclair, Mrs L V Skeats, David George Skeet, Mrs Smith, Mrs G C Smith, Mrs S K Smith, Mrs G Soameson, Mrs Jo Stables, Elizabeth Stacke, Mr M G Stevens, Mary L Stokes, S J Stonier, Joan Storrar, Brian M Stratton, H W Sumpner, Anne Sutcliffe, Gloria M Sutcliffe, Mrs A Swanbury, Mrs K Sweet, Mrs E Swinton, Mrs F Sykes, Roger Sykes, Joan Tailby, Adrian Talbot, Mrs B R Taylor, Dr W G Taylor, Mrs Joyce B Thompson, Darryl Thomson, Mrs V Thorley, Angela Timms, Dave Tolfree, Hanna Tomczewska,

Ackowledgements

Mrs Susan Truscott, Mrs E Turner, Mrs Patricia
Turner, Bert Twiddy, Irene Tyson, Mrs Rachel
Ufton, Mr R Dudley Utting, L Vale, Barbara
Verdie, Mr G Wagstaff, Penelope Walford, Mrs
G M Walker, Mrs P Walker, W R Walsh, Jane
Ward, Anthony Warner, Melanie Warwick,
E Watkins, Mrs M Watson, Angela Watts, Mrs
Maureen Wayman, Mrs Weir, Bernard Wells,
Mrs L Wesley, Mrs S B Weston, Mrs A Whatford,
Mrs J R White, T H White, Tony Whitmarsh,
Mrs D Whittle, Mrs J Whiteley, Mrs F Wilkins,
Mrs Mary R Wilkinson, Mrs R F Wilkinson,
Barbara Willett, Mrs D Leslie Williams, Glenis
Williams, Audrey Wilson, Kazuko Wood,
B Woodwark, Jill Worth, Jill Wren, Marion Wren,
Mrs C Wright, Mickie Wynne-Davies,
M Yannicosta, Mrs J Young, Mrs S Young,
Mrs Susan Young, Mrs Ghulam Zohra.

∽

Every effort has been made by the Publishers and
The Daily Telegraph to contact each individual
contributor. If any tip has appeared without
proper acknowledgement, the Publishers and
The Daily Telegraph apologize unreservedly.
Please address any queries to the editor, c/o
the Publishers.

Index

Index

Index